TOLKIEN, EUROPE,
AND TRADITION

All countries that no longer have legends will
be condemned to die of cold.

— Patrice de la Tour du Pin,
La Quête de joie, 1933

Very great poets have learned — this is their duty given that
humanity has not created new myths — to bring types of the
fable to life with inspiration and to make them young again
with a modern vision.

— Stéphane Mallarmé,
Les dieux antiques, 1880

They'll come back, those gods you're always crying about!
Time will bring back the order of the old days.

— Gérard de Nerval, 'Delfica',
Les Chimères, 1854

ARMAND BERGER

Tolkien, Europe, and Tradition

FROM CIVILISATION TO THE DAWN OF IMAGINATION

ARKTOS
LONDON 2022

Tolkien, l'Europe et la tradition: La civilisation à l'aune de l'imaginaire, published by La Nouvelle Librairie éditions in 2022.

The series *Foundations* is the result of a cooperation between Arktos Media and the Institut Iliade (Paris). The French original is published in the series 'Collection Longue Mémoire de l'Institut Iliade'.

ISBN	978-1-914208-97-3 (Paperback)
	978-1-914208-98-0 (Ebook)
TRANSLATION	Jason Rogers
EDITING	Constantin von Hoffmeister
COVER & LAYOUT	Tor Westman

🌐 Arktos.com　　🅵 fb.com/Arktos　　✈ @arktosmedia　　🅾 arktosmedia

CONTENTS

A Brief Note on This Translation vii

Introduction ix

I. In Search of a Lost Mythology 1
   Itinerary of an *Amans Linguarum*   1
   Readings, between Tributes and Excesses   4
   Mythologies of Northwest Europe   8

II. Imagination or the Praise of Tradition 13
   The Mythological Crisis   13
   The Morning Star   15
   The Original Couple   16
   Friend of the Elves   18
   Imagination and Its Traditional Air   20

III. Conceiving a New Heroism 23
   Anglo-Saxon Heroism   23
   Aragorn, or Royal Heroism   25
   The Courage of the Hobbits   27

IV. For an Ecology of Imagination. 31
   The Sense of Nature in Anglo-Saxon Poetry   31
   The Submersion of Númenor or the Other Atlantis   32
   The Technical Alienation of Isengard   35
   The Happy Medium of the Hobbits   38

V. As a Defence of European Civilisation 41
   The Fall of the City   43
   For an Ultimate Rebirth   45

Bibliography for Further Reading 47

L'Institut Iliade for Long European Memory. 48

A BRIEF NOTE ON
THIS TRANSLATION

HIS WORK, originally written in French, offers translations of ancient and modern texts in French — many provided by the author himself — and some are translations of original English texts (Tolkien's letters and citations from *The Lord of the Rings*, for example). Our English edition has provided the original English texts in all instances where an English text was cited and provides modern English translations from other experts for texts that were from non-English sources. Occasionally I have found it necessary to provide fresh translations in order to support the author's arguments, namely a piece from Horace's Latin *Odes* and a few lines of Old English.

Berger's work also cites several French scholars; these citations are in turn translated by me and are not from other published English translations.

Terms related to Middle-earth are rendered as Tolkien himself used them, including the plural of dwarf as *dwarves*. Likewise, when referring to the various races of Middle-earth, these are capitalised as was Tolkien's general practice: Men, Dwarves, Ents, Elves, etc.

The author's notes in the text are offered as standard footnotes; the translator's notes are distinguished by beginning with *Trans. note*.

This work, given its erudition and use of many ancient texts, provided an exciting and enjoyable challenge that I thoroughly loved. Any mistakes or errors are my own.

JASON ROGERS

INTRODUCTION

T IS THE SIGNATURE privilege of man to collect within his bosom all the weight of his tradition and to let it escape, much like a censer, giving off the sweet bouquet of incense when it is released. For it is in 'an eternal novelty, which forms the grandiose elements of the past', as Goethe said, that the long immemorial chain is maintained, in the passing down of our spiritual and civilisational heritage. The filial aspect holds the sacred; thus, youth attains a new sensation. But its flame must be maintained so that it does not fade away in the subtle gold hues of evening where the wolf roams! Let it remain upright and intact! Never tire of keeping vigil over the epic of its ancestors! Inevitable is the day when it must take charge of its destiny.

Like Dante, along with Virgil and Beatrice, surveying super-earthly kingdoms, it belongs to those young souls, to generations yet to come, to travel to lands that are still unknown to them, steeped in tales and legends, which transmit a wisdom that gets to the very essence of life, out of the difficulties and complications created by modern society. In this, the universe invented by the writer John Ronald Reuel Tolkien offers an authentic re-enchantment of the world, as ancient traditions once did. This contemporary epic occupies a fundamental place in the mental universe of today's European, in that its author was greatly inspired by European traditions and their founding texts: the *Iliad*, *Beowulf*, the *Eddas*, as well as the *Kalevala*. Continents falling within a vast civilisational space and in the long term to be rediscovered in a new form. And now we are engaged in this adventure, understood as a stroll along the intersection of the real, the mythical, and the imaginary.

IN SEARCH OF A LOST MYTHOLOGY

T THE TURN OF the 19th century, the literati reached a critical state: they believed that they had already said and studied everything there was to say and study. 'The flesh is sad, alas! And I have read all the books', Mallarmé said. This era of upheaval worked like a mirror of the post-war era. But, beyond these divides, there remained authors who thought backwards, towards ancient traditions. Tolkien is one of them.

Itinerary of an *Amans Linguarum*[1]

Tolkien's career lay in originality. Above all, he was someone who was driven by a deep desire to know languages, a decisive love that gives his literary work a colour never seen elsewhere: that of musicality; a constant euphony of imagination, thought up to its last detail, which resonates in us at every moment with enthusiasm.

---

1   Trans. note: *Amans linguarum*, Latin for 'lover of languages'.

John Ronald Reuel Tolkien was born on 2 January 1892 in Free Orange State, a former province of South Africa.[2] During a stay in England with his mother Mabel and his younger brother Hilary, he received the news that his father Arthur, who had remained in Africa, had died. Since this took place in 1896, there was no question of going back to Africa.

Tolkien was a little boy who had a gift for languages. He learned French, German, and Latin from his mother. In grammar school and secondary school, he discovered ancient Greek, Old and Middle English, as well as Gothic and Norse. He was also introduced to Welsh. At Oxford, he studied classics. Though the young Tolkien took up Greek and Latin with ease — he even occasionally conducted student debates in the language of Cicero — his first love for the classical authors began to wane. However, his interest in historical linguistics, a discipline in which he excelled, remained intact. He then changed his curriculum, going into English studies with Norse as a speciality. The young student at the time — sometime in the 1910s — flourished fully in the in-depth study of language and literature.

Outside his studies, Tolkien had cultivated a 'secret vice'[3] since his childhood, that of inventing languages. It was not just a hobby, as we find among bright children even today. It was more a creative feat nurtured by deep determination, for Tolkien had not merely outlined some linguistic babble. As it grew, and as the influence of certain real languages became more important, each time he created a new speech, the search for the right sounds, a coherent vocabulary, and an increasingly complex grammatical structure became powerful challenges. In his youth, he developed *Animalic*, *Nephbosh*, and *Naffarin* — witnesses to the fragmentary state of a true hobby, which was by no means futile.

---

2   Trans. note: Free Orange State was an independent Boer republic under the British Crown in Southern Africa. It became a province after the British victory in the Second Boer War in 1902.

3   A phrase taken from a lecture he gave in 1931, which deals with these invented languages, as well as with the links between languages and mythologies.

Around 1910, Tolkien discovered the Gothic tongue, the old-est written Germanic language, whose main literary witness is the Bible, translated by Bishop Wulfila in the 4th century of our era. He was totally caught up in Gothic, to the point that he started to invent additional words to fill the gaps in the surviving vocabulary by recon-structing proto-words through a comparison of Germanic languages. He proceeded in the same way that specialists in Indo-European did in the 19th century: artificially reconstructing words according to ob-served laws of language change. Tolkien's project was quite ambitious and he ventured fairly far into it. He even wrote a poem in this 'neo-Gothic' language, published in *Songs for the Philologists* (1936) and titled 'Bagmē Blōma', 'Flower of the Trees'. With this poem, Tolkien tried to reconstitute a Germanic *Urpoesie*[4], which, beyond mere cre-ation for the sake of pleasure, was really understood as a rebirth of a Gothic poetry that was unfortunately lost.

Perhaps Tolkien saw the limits of such a goal. So, he had to cul-tivate his love of languages in a new way. Reading the *Kalevala*, a body of Finnish heroic-mythological tales collected by the folklorist Elias Lönnrot throughout the 19th century, made quite an impact on him. The text is composed in a speech of superb sonority: Finnish, a non-Indo-European language, but one which had very early con-tacts — probably several centuries before our era — with Germanic languages. Tolkien described his encounter with this language in terms of wine: 'It was like discovering a complete wine-cellar filled with bottles of an amazing wine of a kind and flavour never tasted before. It quite intoxicated me.'[5] Finnish had a decisive influence on Tolkien. He then left his Germanic language to build from scratch

4   Trans. note: An *Urpoesie* is something like an ancient poetry that does not align with modern metres and rhyme.

5   Humphrey Carpenter (ed.), *The Letters of J. R. R. Tolkien*, Houghton Mifflin Company, copyright 1981 by George Allen & Unwin (Publishers) Ltd. Letter no. 163. [Trans. note: As Tolkien's letters are referred to often in this work, from here on we will refer to this publication simply as 'Tolkien, *Letters*'.]

Quenya, which he would not cease to elaborate and fine-tune throughout his life. Tolkien went even further: he created families of languages — like Indo-European languages — to integrate *Quenya* into a wider linguistic landscape. Being realistic was obligatory. The languages invented by Tolkien within his *Legendarium* — about forty or so, more or less, essentially draw their inspiration from our ancient European languages.

Readings, between Tributes and Excesses

Tolkien is said to have read all the books essential to his intellectual formation around the age of twenty. We should believe it, given that the young man's erudition aroused such admiration and respect. During the First World War, Tolkien fought at the Battle of the Somme; he was, as Maurice Genevoix would say, among *Ceux de 14*.[6] In this fratricidal conflict, he lost his dearest friends, although he himself got out after contracting trench fever. Emerging from this heartbreak, after a long convalescence, he had to work to earn a living. Between 1919 and 1920, he was an assistant lexicographer for the *Oxford English Dictionary* and was responsible for writing word entries under the letter *W*. The extent of his philological knowledge was impressive, according to Henry Bradley, the dictionary's director: 'His work gives evidence of an unusually thorough mastery of Anglo-Saxon and of the facts and principles of the comparative grammar of the Germanic languages. Indeed, I have no hesitation in saying that I have never known a man of his age who was in these respects his equal.'[7] One example among others of his knowledge, again taken from philology.

---

6   Trans. note: Genevoix's title *Ceux de 14* refers to 'those of 1914', that is, those men who were the first ones to see combat at the beginning of the First World War in July of 1914.

7   Carpenter, Humphrey, *Tolkien: A Biography*, Houghton Mifflin Company Boston, 1977, p. 100.

Tolkien developed a pronounced taste for reading when he was very young, which his mother passed down to him. Like many children, he was fond of legends. His imagination was nurtured by the *Fairy Books* of Scottish folklorist Andrew Lang who, at the turn of the 19th century, compiled a collection of ancient wisdom stories for young readers. The story of the hero *Sigurðr*, who receives his ultimate crowning in the work of Richard Wagner, and his struggle with the dragon *Fáfnir*, left a profound imprint on the young Tolkien. Andrew Lang had, beyond dispute, influenced the would-be author of *The Hobbit*.

Tolkien, however, did not share the folklorist's belief that the fairy tale should be intended, or reserved, for children, as if it were 'an accident of our domestic history'.[8] The tale carries four core values: that of leaving the real for a different but believable world, that of achieving wonder, that of complete escape, and that of bringing joy or enthusiasm in the etymological sense of the word, a transport, in the light of a happy ending, a *eucatastrophe* as Tolkien put it. Thus, the fairy tale is not the prerogative of youth, since an adult may also be touched by the effect of reading the fairy tale. It is therefore advisable to reread, with this mature look, the work of Baroness d'Aulnoy, the Brothers Grimm, Charles Perrault, or Hans Christian Andersen.

In English literature, when we speak of *elves*, strange elusive creatures that are straight out of the lower Scandinavian mythology, two names stand out as precursors to Tolkien: William Shakespeare and Lord Dunsany. These two authors have given these fabulous beings a representation that has for several centuries influenced our collective imagination.

The elves may have been linked to the veneration of ancestors, as well as to a cult of fertility and death in the Scandinavian tradition,

---

8   Taken from a lecture, titled 'On Fairy-Stories', given in 1947. [Trans. note: The text of this lecture can be found in multiple places online, including the University of Houston, Texas website: https://uh.edu/fdis/_taylor-dev/ readings/tolkien.html.]

and appear to be related to 'spirits of nature' in the English tradition. Germanic sources also do not exclude the notion that elves are an old class of gods, perhaps elemental deities that were worshiped across the sea or among the forests or hills. But in the central Middle Ages, the representation of the elves evolved. In Scandinavia, they are turned into demons with the advent of Christianity, and have more or less fallen into oblivion at the threshold of modern times, like a hidden people (*huldufólk*) that one can hardly see. The same became true of elves within German folk beliefs. But there would be a major shift in England in the way the elf figure was represented during the late Middle Ages, focusing more on the bright and positive side of the elves, as Shakespeare's Oberon can be seen in *A Midsummer Night's Dream*.

It is from this more recent English tradition that these elvish beings, now more fantasy and fairy-like, re-entered German space during the modern era, and especially in the 18th century, through the influence of poets, including Johann Gottfried Herder. This is where in the 19th century, again in England, the delicate, barely visible, winged creatures that abound in children's books are born. Let us remember that idyllic representation of Leconte de Lisle in the famous refrain of his poem 'Les Elfes', published in the collection *Poèmes barbares*:

Couronnés de thym et de marjolaine, Les Elfes joyeux dansent sur la plaine.[9]

On this point, among many others, Tolkien had a profound disagreement with Shakespeare's vision. He thus refers to the use of the word *elf* as 'a disastrous debasement of this word, in which Shakespeare played an unforgiveable part, has really overloaded it with regrettable tones, which are too much to overcome'.[10] It is true that the 'immortal bard', as Isaac Asimov put it, had drawn from many European myths

---

9   Trans. note: 'Crowned with thyme and marjoram, the merry elves dance on the plain.'

10   Tolkien, *Letters*, no. 151.

and legends with the aim of creating a work that would exceed his sources of inspiration, and which, in turn, nurtured our European imagination for a long time.[11] In this way we receive the character of Hamlet from Shakespeare, although Hamlet comes straight out of the *Gesta Danorum* of Saxo Grammaticus.

But Tolkien's hard criticism comes not only from the man as a writer; the philologist and the mythologist are never far away. His knowledge of Germanic traditions allowed him to go beyond this Shakespearean imagery that has been around for centuries. He made Elves, in his universe, the most powerful beings, gifted in magic and in the arts, endowed with immortality as well as great beauty. True, Tolkien's conception of the Elves was not identical to the Scandinavian tradition in any way, but his is the one that came closest.

Less known, however, is the legacy of Lord Dunsany. Roughly contemporary with Tolkien, Dunsany was also a multifaceted writer. His best-known novel, *The King of Elfland's Daughter* (1924), recounts the romantic relationship between a human prince and an elf princess, on the border of the real and the imaginary. The parallel with Tolkien is striking in that Dunsany invented detailed and autonomous universes from their mythical foundation to an advanced era, all composed in a style at once mediaeval, Hellenistic, and Celtic. According to Tolkien, he was one of those writers of English literature who were 'inventors of names' (along with Swift, or Carrol and his 'Jabberwocky'), a key criterion in fiction. However, he had reservations about the limit of such an enterprise with Dunsany, which is incomplete and inconsistent. Once again, he is speaking as a philologist.

William Morris was a man of letters who is thought to have had a decisive influence on Tolkien. A member of the Arts and Crafts movement, and close to Pre-Raphaelites like Edward Burne-Jones, Morris was also a fruitful author who left a great impression on Tolkien. This jack-of-all-trades translated the most eminent founding texts of our

---

11 Henri Suhamy, *Shakespeare et l'Europe: Quatre siècles de mémoire vivante*, La Nouvelle Librairie éditions, 2020.

European literature: the *Odyssey*, the *Aeneid*, *Beowulf*, mediaeval French novels and several Icelandic sagas, including the *Völsunga saga*, with the help of Eiríkur Magnússon. At the end of his life, he wrote several novels, including *The House of the Wolfings* (1889), which depicted a glorious Germanic past and admirable Gothic tribes. Tolkien was a devoted reader of Morris's work, to such an extent that he declared in one of his letters his intention to rewrite the story of Kullervo, a tragic hero of the *Kalevala*, 'somewhat on the lines of Morris' romances with chunks of poetry in between'.[12] We still find in many places in Tolkien's *Legendarium* references to Morris, a true testimony of respect for this cantor of the European tradition, whom Tolkien was able to update.

Mythologies of Northwest Europe

Tolkien was someone concerned with the great European mythologies, of which he had an intimate knowledge due to his academic training. His sensibilities, determined by his unexpected and happy encounters, made him turn to the traditions of Northwest Europe: Celtic, Finnish, and German-Scandinavian.

Let us look at Celtic first. The *res celtica* is tricky to understand. It is not uniform, and is stretched out over time — several centuries — and over space, be it geographical or linguistic. Tolkien developed a particular interest in Welsh material. He read carefully the *Mabinogion* text, a compendium in prose of four legendary stories written in Middle Welsh and compiled between the 12th and 13th centuries, from which we sometimes find influences in Tolkien. His Celtic tropism also led him to survey the Breton lays, of which Marie de France is the worthy inheritor.[13] Thus, inspired by this style, he wrote *The Lay of Aotrou and Itroun*, first in 1930, and then a second version in 1941–1942. He

---

12   Tolkien, *Letters*, no. 1.

13   Trans. note: Marie de France's work, twelve short narrative poems, referred to as 'lays', were written in Anglo-Norman French, likely in the 12th century.

also wrote the poem 'Imram', published in 1955, which draws on the Irish tradition of initiatory journeys, and which is based on the most famous of them, *The Voyage of Saint Brendan*.

We must still mention, in relation to Celtic material, the interesting comparison between Tolkien's Elves and the Tuatha Dé Danann of Irish mythology. Using the theories of Georges Dumézil, as applied to the Celts by Françoise Le Roux and Christian-Joseph Guyonvarc'h, while studying Celtic civilisation — of a social, military, religious or even magical nature — through mythological texts, one can draw fruitful parallels with the stories of Middle-earth. One thinks of Valinor, the Undying Lands depicted in *The Silmarillion*, which recall *Tír na nÓg*, the Celtic paradise. Tolkien, too, rearranged the Arthurian material that he knew so well — notably through *Sir Gawain and the Green Knight* — in an alliterative poem published a few years ago: *The Fall of Arthur*.[14]

Now on to Finnish. The material from Finland was gathered by Lönnrot in the 19th century in a collection called the *Kalevala*. The work appears to be comprised of texts from various sources. There are myths, legends, hero stories, epics, and even lyrical stories. The traditional background is Finno-Ugric, and the composite story addresses the classic themes of pre-Christian traditions, such as the metamorphosis of animals into human beings, the appearance of monsters, and the evocation of magic. It also tells the story of a sacred object with immense powers, the *sampo*, and of heroes who set out in search of it, a quest for power but also for meaning. The *Kalevala* is, in many ways, a reflection on power, one that resembles the quest of the Silmarils or that of the Ring in Tolkien.

Tolkien was inspired by the *Kalevala* tradition in several respects. In particular, the story of Kullervo, a tragic hero, influenced him. Between 1912 and 1916, he composed a rewriting of this narrative. This material, which he liked so much, would be used in the history

---

14 Trans. note: Tolkien's *The Fall of Arthur* was published posthumously in 2013.

of Túrin Turambar as it appears in *The Silmarillion*, as well as in his development of *The Children of Húrin*.

And finally German-Scandinavian. It goes without saying that it is to this tradition that the most beautiful part belongs. The *res germanica* is omnipresent in Tolkien's work and it would be futile to attempt to speak on it exhaustively here.[15] However, let us offer in this little booklet several Germanic insights that highlight this importance.

One of these works, after all, left a strong impression on Tolkien: the *Völsunga saga*, probably written around 1260 in Iceland. The narrative draws the main elements of its history from the *Eddas*, from the heroic poems, the contents of which the *Völsunga* reworks in prose form. The Norse text was similarly inspired by songs that are lost, and reported events that are not an integral part of the cycle of primitive legends. Somewhere between continuity of tradition and literary invention, this masterpiece is a privileged testimony to the mythology of ancient Scandinavians, as well as a text of primary importance for the study of the *Nibelungen* epic.

The saga is a strange and glorious tale. Tolkien wrote that the *Völsunga* 'tells of the oldest of treasure hunts: the quest of the red gold of Andvari, the dwarf. It tells of the brave Sigurd Fafnirsbane, who was cursed by the possession of this gold, who, in spite of his greatness, had no happiness from his love for Brynhild'.[16] Tolkien, as we mentioned above, discovered this story in Lang's children's books. In the same 1911 paper cited above, he said that '[i]t shows us the highest epic genius struggling out of savagery into complete and conscious humanity. Though inferior to Homer in most respects, though as a whole the Northern epic has not the charm and delight of the Southern, yet in a

---

15   See Rudolf Simek, *Mittelerde: Tolkien und die germanische Mythologie*, C. H. Beck, 2005. See also Armand Berger, 'Tolkien le philologue et la *res germanica*', *J. R. R. Tolkien, Nouvelle École*, no. 70, 2021, p. 15–31.

16   From a paper read to the Literary Society on the Norse Sagas on 17 February 1911; a summary of which was published in the *King Edward's School Chronicle* in March 1911. Citation available at https://muse.jhu.edu/article/389576.

certain bare veracity it excels it, and also in the story of the Volsungs in the handling of the love interest.'[17]

---

[17] Trans. note: Ibid.

CHAPTER II

IMAGINATION OR THE PRAISE OF TRADITION

O BE FULLY IMMERSED in one's culture, to the point that an unstoppable *furor* spreads within one's self. A powerful impetus that seeks to give new breath to a tradition that is fragmented, if not already lost. Thus was Tolkien's ambitious plan to create a 'mythology for England'.

The Mythological Crisis

When Tolkien was introduced to philology and mythology, it soon became clear to him that England, although an heir to our European civilisation, lacked the kind of authentic tradition that man naturally feels drawn to connect to. Germany has its *Nibelungenlied*, Italy has its *Commedia*, and France has its *Chanson de Roland*. But what about England? *Beowulf*, you might say, that masterpiece of mediaeval Anglo-Saxon literature. Of course, this 'heroic elegy' is English in terms of its own language, but not in terms of its traditional background, which is purely Scandinavian. The plot takes place in Denmark and southern Sweden, the hero belongs to the *Geat* tribe, and many of its motifs are found in Norse literature. What can one do? Contemplate in bitterness that one's land does not have a found-ing story, a banner of identity?

Tolkien looked further. In an Old English Christian poem with a stylistic similarity to *Beowulf* and which recounts the *Exodus* in epic form, he comments at length on the word *Sigelhearwan*, 'Ethiopians'. In this etymological investigation, he comes up with a hypoth-esis — with all the reservations that scientific rigor imposes — that this term originally referred to the Scandinavian fire giants of Múspell, a part of *Ragnarök*, the eschatological narrative of Scandinavian tradi-tion.[1] Thus stanza 52 of the *Völuspá*, the most prominent poem of the commonly called *Poetic Edda*:

> Surt fares from the south | with the scourge of branches,
> The sun of the battle gods | shone from his sword;
> The crags are sundered, | the giant-women sink,
> The dead throng hel-way, | and heaven is cloven.[2]

While this idea of a pre-Christian reminiscence is appealing, it is nonetheless a conjecture. Moreover, we still have again the same prob-lem found in *Beowulf*, namely that we are talking once again about a tradition that is not English.

The problem seems insoluble, and philology unfortunately offers few convincing results. This is due both to history and to successive waves of invasions (Celtic, Saxon, Viking, Norman) of the country. Several European traditions have trodden this English soil. Add to that a Christian varnish that hardly allows a man who is an heir of this tradition to get hold of a clearly defined base. Tolkien talks about this identity problem in a long letter in 1951: 'I was from early days grieved by the poverty of my own beloved country: it had no stories

---

1   J. R. R. Tolkien, 'Sigelwara Land', *Medium Ævum*, vol. 1.3, December 1932, pp. 183–196 and *Medium Ævum*, vol. 3.2, June 1934, pp. 95–111.

2   Trans. note: We reproduce here the translation of Henry Adams Bellows; *The Poetic Edda*, Princeton University Press, 1936. There exist multiple reprints by various publishers. https://www.sacred-texts.com/neu/poe/poe03.htm.

of its own (bound up with its tongue and soil), not of the quality that I sought, and found (as an ingredient) in legends of other lands. There was Greek, and Celtic, and Romance, Germanic, Scandinavian, and Finnish (which greatly affected me); but nothing English...'[3] Tolkien continues, further recalling his original intention to give England a mythology: 'But once upon a time (my crest has long since fallen) I had in mind to make a body of more or less connected legend, ranging from the large and cosmogonic, to the level of romantic fairy-story... Which I could dedicate simply to: England; to my country. It should possess the tone and quality that I desired, somewhat cool and clear, be redolant of our "air" (the clime and soil of the North West, meaning Britain and the hither parts of Europe: not Italy or the Aegean, still less the East)...'[4]

The Morning Star

But how far back does such a project date with Tolkien? Mediaeval English literature can provide us with some answers. In an Anglo-Saxon religious work, *Crist I*, probably composed at the end of the 8th century, Tolkien, while he was a student, discovered two verses that hit him:

> *Eala Earendel engla beorhtast / Ofer middangeard monnum sended*
> Hail, Earendel, brightest of angels / Sent unto people over Middle-earth[5]

The word *earendel* means 'morning star' in Old English, and is based on an Indo-European root — *$h2eusos$-, 'dawn', 'east' — , whose verbal form *$h2wes$- means 'to become bright', 'to dawn'. *Earendel* poses difficulties in the area of etymology. The root of the word goes back to the common Germanic *Auzawandilaz*, 'the luminous wandering', and has cognates in many ancient Germanic languages. Such a name

3   Tolkien, *Letters*, no. 131.
4   Ibid.
5   Trans. note: Translation mine.

might refer to an auroral myth, unfortunately lost, possibly related to Venus.

This gap in tradition Tolkien decided to fill by writing, in the summer of 1914, 'The Voyage of Eärendel the Evening Star', the story of a sailor traversing the heavenly worlds on his skiff, a strong flash launched from the harbours of the Sun. This story lays the foundation for Tolkien's fictional mythology. The auroral light, central in European religions,[6] is what indicates the author's intent concerning our civilisational enclosure.

The Original Couple

As in most traditions, Tolkien also offered a creation story of the universe and of the creatures that live there. In a primitive version of the story of the awakening of men — it appears in a very different way in *The Silmarillion* — the author establishes a subtle link between his mythology and those of the Germanic, if not all Indo-European, peoples. It is mentioned in 'Gilfanon's Tale' in *The Book of Lost Tales*. The first beings, awakened, are called *Ermon* and *Elmir*. In a note, Christopher Tolkien, the writer's son, who was in charge of publishing his father's later texts, indicates that above the name Ermon Tolkien annotated on his text the Old English word *æsc*, 'ash'.

One sees the relationship with the Norse word *Askr*, which in Scandinavian tradition is the name given to the first man; he and his wife *Embla* — which means 'elm' or 'vine' — were shaped from two trees found on the shore. Note stanzas 17 and 18 of the *Völuspá*:

> 17. Then from the throng | did three come forth,
> From the home of the gods, | the mighty and gracious;
> Two without fate | on the land they found,
> Ask and Embla, | empty of might.
> 18. Soul they had not, | sense they had not,

---

6   Jean Haudry, *La religion cosmique des Indo-Européens*, Archè/Les Belles Lettres, 1987.

Heat nor motion, | nor goodly hue;
Soul gave Othin, | sense gave Hönir,
Heat gave Lothur | and goodly hue.[7]

Perhaps the name *Ermon* is reminiscent of the ash tree Yggdrasil, the *axis mundi et universalis columna* of Scandinavian cosmogony. The *Völuspá* continues with the following stanza:

19. An ash I know, | Yggdrasil its name,
With water white | is the great tree wet;
Thence come the dews | that fell in the dales,
Green by Urth's well | does it ever grow.[8]

The resemblance seems obvious, especially if one takes note of the name of the plant-like axis in continental Germanic: *Irminsul*, which we, like Jan de Vries, translate with 'great column',[9] which is described as the Saxon holy place that Charlemagne had destroyed during the invasion of 772.

The name *Irmin* appears under the pen of the monk Widukind of Corvey in *Res gestae Saxonicae* (968). The Saxons, having won a victory over the Thuringians, celebrated their triumph with a remarkable act: they erected an altar at the eastern gate of the city they had taken. This altar had the shape of a column representing Hercules and bearing the name of the god Mars, *Hirmin* according to the chronicler, which he approximates to the Greek *Hermis*, or Hermes. Although his likening of *Hirmin* to the Greco-Roman gods is of no value, Widukind's testimony is important and the link with *Irminsul* is beyond obvious. The name of *Irmin* is also that of a Germanic people. In his *Germania*, Tacitus states that the three great confederations of

7   Trans. note: Henry Adams Bellows, *The Poetic Edda*, Princeton University Press, 1936. Multiple reprints by various publishers. https://www.sacred-texts.com/neu/poe/poe03.htm.

8   Ibid.

9   Jan de Vries, 'La valeur religieuse du mot germanique Irmin', *Cahiers du Sud*, no. 314, July 1952, pp. 18–27.

Germania included the *Ingævones*, the *Herminones*, and the *Istævones*, names given after the three sons of *Mannus*, 'man'.[10]

Finally, there is the thorny question of whether there was a Germanic god named *Irmin*. One cannot decide, but comparisons with the Indo-Iranian god Aryaman[11], as Georges Dumézil put it in *Le troisième souverain*,[12] suggest that there could have existed, in the Germanic pantheon, a third sovereign who could have been filled by such a god, if he had existed. In his book, Dumézil compares Aryaman with Eremon, a figure of Irish mythology, who was the first king of Ireland after its conquest by his sons. Concerning Eremon, he writes that 'he is *king* in the same way that Mitra and Varuna were: he joins them functionally in that he played the same role, that *of introducing a new settlement...* Finally, linked undoubtedly to the word *aire* (**aryak-*), this Eremon was the one who founded the Irish people of history (according to this tradition) and was different — and later — than the ancient Irish who were connected to the gods, the Tûatha Dé Dânann, those who existed "before history"'.[13]

The link between the Irish Eremon and Tolkien's Ermon is therefore clear: both are at the origin of a new race, that of men. These parallels between Tolkien's work and the European mythological foundation are not mere coincidences. This is clearly an intentional attempt by Tolkien to tie his mythology to Germanic and Celtic traditions.

Friend of the Elves

The study of a 'mythology for England' cannot be complete without taking into account the story of Ælfwine, 'friend of the elves' in Old

---

10 Tacitus, *Germania*. Berger uses J. Perret's French translation, Les Belles Lettres, 1949, p. 71.

11 Trans. note: Aryaman is the god of Aryan society.

12 Georges Dumézil, *Le troisième souverain: Essai sur le dieu indo-iranien Aryaman et sur la formation de l'histoire mythique de l'Irlande*, G. P. Maisonneuve, 1949.

13 Ibid., pp. 170–171.

English, who makes appearances throughout Tolkien's *Legendarium* in several unfinished works. This character appears in *The Lost Tales* (roughly 1916). He evolves and is also found in *The Lost Road* (1937) and *The Notion Club Papers* (roughly 1945). We shall try to create a coherent picture of him.

Ælfwine, the son of Eadwine, was an Anglo-Saxon born around 869, living in Britain in the 10th century. When he was nine years old, his father took to the sea with his ship *Éarendel* and never returned. The Danes were carrying out attacks in England. Ælfwine fled with his mother towards the west of Welsh country. He was a distant descendant of Eärendil, and had, like all members of this lineage, a passion for the sea. He learned Welsh, the art of sailing, and, in adulthood, returned to England to serve Odda, a thane of King Eadweard. Ælfwine travelled often and took an interest in seafaring stories. He thus heard Irish legends like that of Saint Brendan or of Máel Dúin, both of whom took to the sea and reached wonderful islands. Eventually, Ælfwine wants to go west one day, toward those legendary lands. So, he leaves for Ireland, accompanied by one of his friends. But fatigue overcomes them and a dreamlike death seems to take hold of them. When Ælfwine wakes up, he is lying on a beach in Tol Eressëa and a group of Elves brings his ship back to the shore. He arrives at Tavrobel where Pengolodh lives, who tells him the *Ainulindalë*, the story of creation, and shows him the books containing the greatest stories of the world, like the *Quenta Silmarillion*. Ælfwine feeds on this knowledge. When he returns to England, he translates *The Silmarillion* and many other works into Old English.

To truly grasp the author's intention, it is necessary to read the original version of this narrative in *The Lost Tales*, which holds many riches. What is important to remember is that Ælfwine is the depository of an authentic Elf tradition, and Tolkien's plan to create a mythology for England as a project was not abandoned in 1910; his version of *The Lost Road* confirms this. Moreover, if the English geographical and mythological elements are evident in the history of Ælfwine, the role of this character, as a translator of Elvish legends into Old English, shows that the linguistic element, in the intention of creating a mythology, is essential, to such a point that Tolkien demonstrates the coexistence, for a time, of Old English and the Elvish tongues in his mythology, as well as their kinship within the *Legendarium*.

Imagination and Its Traditional Air

The mythological attempts we have just mentioned have to do with unfinished works of Tolkien, which have little connection with the *Legendarium* as we know it through *The Silmarillion, The Hobbit,* and *The Lord of the Rings*. Because his plan to give England a mythology was without a doubt overly ambitious, Tolkien sought another way to think of myth. This new way of thinking was expressed in two different ways.

The first consisted in rewriting tales and legends that Tolkien liked. He thus wrote *The Fall of Arthur*, repeating part of the Arthurian cycle, and gave life to the heroes of the North in *The Legend of Sigurd and Gudrún,* which uses the traditional background of the *Völsunga saga* and several songs of the *Edda*. Tolkien also reworked a tragic character from the *Kalevala* in *The Story of Kullervo*. He rewrote *The Lay of Aotrou and Itroun*, recalling in this work the Breton Lays, as well as 'Sellic Spell', a story that tells Beowulf's life in the way of the folklorists, inspired in this by the tale of Jean de l'Ours.

The second, more well-known, was the admirable effort to breathe mythological material from different European traditions into his literary work. *The Lord of the Rings* is the perfect example of this. By doing it this way, Tolkien cast an extremely bright light on the slopes of our creative imagination and ultimately on the deepest structures of our culture. Myth, with its procession of traditional thoughts, although attenuated by the original project, is not absent. It survives in fragments and occasionally manages to mix with Christian feelings that impart to it a new vitality just as it imparts to them an even more dramatic, unknown force. Imagination brings the support of the senses to the work of reason; it transforms into creation what would otherwise remain pure vision. However, the fusion of these principles of inspiration is so intimate that, far from there being any antagonism between them, the increase in strength of any one of them immediately increases that of the others: the higher moral inspiration rises, the more alive myth becomes, and the more intense realism becomes. It is through these two approaches that the author's intention is understood: to present to modern man a vast fresco of ancient times through remodelled traditions.

CHAPTER III

CONCEIVING A NEW HEROISM

EDIAEVAL LITERATURE for Tolkien occupies a fundamental place. Without it, it is quite clear that his literary work would be of a very different nature, losing for many that particular atmosphere that saturates *The Hobbit* and *The Lord of the Rings*. Tolkien, for example, draws from ancient stories a teaching about heroism that echoes the contemporary heroism of the First World War.

Anglo-Saxon Heroism

Two Old English works are imbued with powerful heroism: 'The Battle of Maldon' and *Beowulf*. The first text is a shining testimony of the vitality of the English heroic and patriotic tradition. This poem recounts the fierce struggle of the Saxon army, led by the Earl of Essex, Byrhtnoth, on 10 or 11 August 991 near Maldon, against the Scandinavian army of Olaf Tryggvason. The latter prevails in a bitter battle. In the debacle, the Earl of Essex, who demonstrates his *ofermod*,[1] his pride, in defiance of the Vikings, succumbs. One of his vassals, his beloved friend

> Ælfwine, then, spoke out and valiantly declared: "Let us call to mind those declarations we often uttered over mead, when from our seat we heroes in hall would put up pledges about tough fighting; now it can be proved who is brave. I am willing to make my lineage known to all, that I was from a substantial family in Mercia. My grandfather was called Ealhelm, a wise nobleman blessed with worldly wealth. The thanes among that people shall not reproach me for my wanting to get out of this army, to make my way home, now that my leader is lying hacked down in battle. To me that is the greatest grief: he was both my kinsman and my lord." (lines 211–224)[2]

This warrior emphasises here the importance of the oath, the given word, which in Germanic societies is primordial, as an ancestral law that governs men in their relationship to honour. *Scutum reliquisse præcipuum flagitium*, 'to have abandoned one's shield is the height of disgrace', writes the Latin historian Tacitus in *Germania*.[3] The glorification of loyalty to a valiant person whose destiny one shares, such is the essence of the Anglo-Saxon epic tradition.

The heroic elegy *Beowulf* achieves these same heights. This poem from the late 7th century, which Tolkien had an intimate knowledge of, exalts with strength and lavish detail the world of heroic virtues, a major theme in Anglo-Saxon literature. A paragon of the spirit that animates the Germanic warrior, Beowulf, the eponymous character, embodies this exemplary figure. The man is endowed with superhuman strength; he is animated by such valour that he never backs

---

1 'Then the earl, because of his extravagant spirit [*ofermod*], yielded too much terrain to a more despicable people', verses 89–90. See also Tolkien's smaller text on this notion of *ofermod* in *The Homecoming of Beorhtnoth Beorhthelm's Son* (1953). [Trans. note: This English edition uses the translation of S. A. J. Bradley in *Anglo-Saxon Poetry*, Everyman's Library, 1982.]

2 Trans. note: S. A. J. Bradley, *Anglo-Saxon Poetry*, Everyman's Library, 1982.

3 Trans. note: *Germania*, section 6, line 6. Loeb Classical Library, translated by M. Hutton, Harvard University Press, 1970, first published 1914.

down, firmly determined to embrace a fate that he knows is fatal and inescapable: 'Providence will ever proceed as it must.'[4] The hero is a reflection of a vision of a world that is deeply rooted in the warrior tradition of the peoples of Northern Europe. By accepting his fate at the twilight of his life, and not detracting from his honour — for that was the ethic of the ancient Germanic — Beowulf reached his *telos*. His tragic death is mourned by his own, who compose a superb ode in memory of his great achievements:

> They wanted to utter their grief, to lament the king, to tell aloud his story and to talk about the man. They praised his heroism and his valorous accomplishments.[5]

Beowulf becomes a myth, and his exemplary courage confers literary immortality on him. In many ways, the poem fully satisfies the usual requirements of the 'prince's mirror', a narrated and heroic exemplification of the ideal aristocratic man. *Beowulf* thus delivers a rich and lively vision of the mentality and aesthetics inherent to the ancient Germans, which fed Tolkien. For example, the character of Théoden embodies this Germanic courage: his perseverance during the Battle of the Pelennor Fields,[6] while the King of Rohan knows that he hastens to his doom, is one of the most remarkable illustrations of this.

Aragorn, or Royal Heroism

The origins that inspired the character of Aragorn and their European anchoring give rise to many interpretations. Aragorn seems elusive in the way that he corresponds to the classic model of the mythological

---

4   Trans. note: S. A. J. Bradley, *Beowulf* in *Anglo-Saxon Poetry*, Everyman's Library, 1982, book VI, line 455.

5   Trans. note: Ibid., lines 3170–3173.

6   This battle calls to mind that of the Catalaunian Plains, described by the Gothic historian Jordanes. In the fight, King Theodoric I dies in circumstances reminiscent of the death of Théoden. See Tom Shippey, *The Road to Middle-Earth*, HarperCollins, 2005, p. 18.

hero. Although born into a royal family, he descends from a line of exiled kings, whose prestigious genealogy dates back almost to the dawn of time. Aragorn is raised in obscurity and does not reveal his true identity until he reaches adulthood. Then he follows a long initiation over the course of innumerable voyages, while secretly protecting his kingdom. He is trained in how to govern, he learns how to handle weapons while serving the men of Rohan and Gondor, and gains wisdom through the teaching of Gandalf, as well as the study of ancient traditions and legends. He falls in love with the half-Elf Arwen, but cannot act on his feelings, focusing his faith beyond this, until he has proven himself and regained his kingdom. In the manner of Hamlet, he is a man of spirit and wisdom, courage and moral strength.

The parallel between Hamlet and Aragorn deserves to be made because the two men share several traits. As mentioned above, Hamlet is derived from Amleth, found in the work of Saxo Grammaticus. In the last lines of the third book of *Gesta Danorum*, the nature of the Danish Prince is depicted in this way:

> O valiant Amleth, and worthy of immortal fame, who being shrewdly armed with a feint of folly, covered a wisdom too high for human wit under a marvellous disguise of silliness! And not only found in his subtlety means to protect his own safety, but also by its guidance found opportunity to avenge his father. By this skilful defence of himself, and strenuous revenge for his parent, he has left it doubtful whether we are to think more of his wit or his bravery.[7]

Aragorn and Amleth both, in the end, manage to recover their throne and kingdom, to restore their lineage to its former glory. That is an inevitable return to the heroism that Gandalf predicted in a letter that he leaves for Frodo under the sign of an inn called The Prancing Pony

---

7   Trans. note: For this passage we provide Oliver Elton's translation of the Latin, published by Norroena Society, New York, 1905; this version is now in the public domain: https://www.gutenberg.org/files/1150/1150-h/1150-h.htm#book3.

in Bree — a letter which is certainly one of the most admirable passages in verse in *The Lord of the Rings*:

> All that is gold does not glitter,
> Not all those who wander are lost;
> The old that is strong does not wither,
> Deep roots are not reached by the frost.
> From the ashes a fire shall be woken,
> A light from the shadows shall spring;
> Renewed shall be blade that was broken,
> The crownless again shall be king.[8]

In order for heroism to come into being, there is often a need, in ancient texts, to resort to exile as a necessary passage of great destiny. The theme of wandering is relatively common in European literature: for example, Ulysses or Aeneas in the Greco-Latin tradition. In the Germanic world, this *topos* is often used, both in Old English literature and in the Norse texts. Thus, among many examples, the story of Olaf Haraldsson, the future saint Olaf, who goes into exile in eastern Scandinavia to return to Norway a better man and to become the king that unites it. Like the great kings of yesteryear, Aragorn is pursued by a fate that inevitably brings him to fulfill his duty: to reclaim his ancestral domain and return to his roots.

The Courage of the Hobbits

In an interview with journalist Lars Gustafsson for the Swedish daily *Dagens Nyheter* on 21 August 1961, Tolkien talks about the nodal point of *The Lord of the Rings* in these terms:

> The story is centred on a small, insignificant hobbit, who will bear total responsibility for the victory of good. It is a tale of responsibility, of someone put to a superhuman test; a message sent us of an indefinite, archaic time in

---

8   Tolkien, *The Fellowship of the Ring*, 2nd ed., Houghton Mifflin, 1965, p. 182.

a bizarre world, but depicted so transparently and clearly that we perceive its validity; the impossibility of taking on responsibility, of being a hero.[9]

The Hobbit in Middle-earth does not belong to history. The Hobbit is made discrete, almost invisible to the eyes of Men. He leads a life in the countryside, cares only to maintain his piece of land. In his very nature, he has no business with history. So lives the Hobbit. There is nothing hero-like at first glance. So why put the Hobbit in a costume that is, in fact, too big for him?

We find ourselves at the end of the Third Age of an old world, where for a long time the Elves have played the leading role. But their time has now run out. What remains in the face of this civilisational 'decline', to borrow Oswald Spengler's phrase? The race of Dwarves, although it was prestigious, has always been marginal. That of Men holds good, but could fall at any time under the weight of the enemy. The Council at the home of the half-Elf Elrond, who seeks a way to destroy the one Ring, identifies the various races that inhabit Middle-earth, but a solution seems impossible. It is then that Frodo Baggins, who has until then carried the Ring since they left the Shire, repeatedly risking his little Hobbit life, suddenly, up against this impossible wall, does something quite unexpected:

> A great dread fell on him, as if he was awaiting the pronouncement of some doom that he had long foreseen and vainly hoped might after all never be spoken... At last with an effort he spoke, and wondered to hear his own words, as if some other will was using his small voice. "I will take the Ring," he said, "though I do not know the way."[10]

---

9   Trans. note: This citation from the 1961 interview with Tolkien is found on the personal blog of Lars Gustafsson, posted by him on 12 February 2012: http://larsgustafssonblog.blogspot.com/2012/02/interview-with-r-r-tolkien-from-oxford.html.

10 Ibid., p. 284.

This moment, a decisive turning point in the wonderful life of the Hobbit,[11] raises quite a few questions. Is this a mark of fate or an act of free will? Ambiguity remains.

Perhaps most importantly, it highlights that the Hobbits, who are taking part in the quest to destroy the Ring, throughout various adventures, are beginning to learn about heroism. This initiation can only be carried out in a master-disciple relationship: Gandalf with Frodo or Pippin, Théoden and Éowyn with Merry, etc. Once Sauron is defeated, the Hobbits finally reach an exceptional destiny. The courage they have shown throughout their journey is manifested one last time during the reconquest of the countryside, devastated by the men of Saruman. This final burst, without the need for outside help, shows that the Hobbits — who also in many ways embody the great sacrifice of 1914, that of the simple trench soldier whose name is unknown — are indeed the unanticipated heroes of history, the ones who forever prevail against the enemy. The Shire-folk, a true originality of *The Lord of the Rings* — who are also illustrated in *The Hobbit* with Bilbo Baggins —, lead to the conception of a new form of the great heroic deed based on traditional elements, while offering to give it a novel colour, which brings all its richness to the story.

---

11   Some commentators of the work have seen in him a messiah figure; others see an Arthurian resurgence: wounded, the Hobbit leaves for Tol Eressëa at the end of this part of the story, like the Celtic king left for Avalon after the Battle of Camlann in order to heal his wounds.

CHAPTER IV

FOR AN ECOLOGY
OF IMAGINATION

The Sense of Nature in Anglo-Saxon Poetry

 F TOLKIEN IS influenced by solar myths — perhaps through reading the works of Max Müller, the father of comparative mythology —, as discussed with *Éarendel,* this is certainly because of the importance of *the sense of nature* as it appears in Old English literature[1] — a contemplative nature, a feeling that will have an abstract and explanatory ethical character, on the one hand, and, on the other, one that will be like a gaze riveted to the moving surface of that which is real. We need only read the powerful mediaeval elegies like the Old English *The Seafarer* to be convinced of this:

> I can tell the true riddle of my own self, and speak of my experiences — how
> I have often suffered times of hardship in days of toil, how I have endured
> cruel anxiety at heart and experienced many anxious lodging-places afloat,
> and the terrible surging of the waves. There the hazardous night-watch has
> often found me at the ship's prow when it is jostling along the cliffs. My
> feet were pinched by the cold, shackled by the frost in cold chains, whilst

1   See Émile Pons, *Le thème et le sentiment de la nature dans la poésie anglo-saxonne,* a publication of the faculty of letters at the University of Strasbourg, 1925.

anxieties sighed hot about my heart. Hunger tore from within at the mind of one wearied by the ocean.[2]

The sea — a cold, deep beauty — rises gigantic and terrible before the man doomed to death; it is during times like these that man feels most concerned about his existence, and these songs full of melancholy, like a funeral dirge before the final hour, remind us with the greatest lyricism of our human condition. Such a flowering of simple and pro-found feelings would not be encountered again before the age of ro-manticism, restless yet confident, full of trouble and fervour, towards the end of the 18th century. In such circumstances we think of Charles Baudelaire's verse: 'Free man, ever will you cherish the sea!'[3] In its way of depicting the sea, English literature of the Middle Ages gives the feeling of nature its expressive power by developing it to a very high level, with all its potentialities.

The Submersion of Númenor or the Other Atlantis

Then Manwë upon the Mountain called upon Ilúvatar, and for that time the Valar laid down their government of Arda. But Ilúvatar showed forth his power, and he changed the fashion of the world; and a great chasm opened in the sea between Númenor and the Deathless Lands, and the waters flowed down into it, and the noise and smoke of the cataracts went up to heaven, and the world was shaken.[4] (*The Silmarillion*, Akallabêth)

Tolkien attaches great importance to the sea worlds in *The Silmarillion*, much more so than in *The Hobbit* or *The Lord of the Rings*. The theme of water, as it appears in this work, often harkens back to motifs in

---

2   Trans. note: Bradley, *The Seafarer* in *Anglo-Saxon Poetry*, Everyman's Library, 1982, lines 1–12.

3   Trans. note: From Charles Baudelaire's poem 'L'Homme et la Mer' (Man and the Sea) in his collection *Les Fleurs du mal*. Translation mine.

4   Tolkien, *The Silmarillion*, Houghton Mifflin, 1977, pp. 278–279.

the European tradition. Here is a perfect example. According to the account of 'The Elder Days', the mariner Eärendil sails the skies aboard *Vingilot*, a ship that reminds us of the *Guingelot*, the boat of Wade, a Germanic hero — perhaps a giant of the sea — of whom little is known. This name appears twice in the work of Geoffrey Chaucer, the great English author of the 14th century, and in particular in 'The Merchant's Tale'. Tolkien knew these passages and contributed to Chaucerian literature by publishing landmark studies in philology,[5] by composing a poem in Middle English ('Þe Clerkes Compleinte') as a pastiche of Chaucer, and by working on a poetic and prose anthology of Chaucer, an unfinished work.[6]

Wade is also attested in other places in the Germanic tradition: in 'Widsith', one of the oldest Old English poems, the name appears in a *þula*, an enumeration of kings and princes. Here he reigns over the Helsingas, a people assumed to be of Scandinavian origin. In mediaeval German literature, the character shows up in *The Book of Verona*, a long poem that tells of the adventures of Dietrich von Bern — who is none other than Theodoric, the king of the Ostrogoths —, a hero of the *Nibelungenlied,* who is found in a number of Germanic texts. Under the name of Vadi, Wade appears in the *Þiðrekssaga af Bern*, a Norse adaptation of Dietrich's great deeds.[7] *The Book of Verona* and its Scandinavian version present Wade as the father of Wayland, also known as Wieland or Völundr, the blacksmith god of northern tradition, whose story, according to the *Völundarkviða* — one of the heroic songs of the *Edda* — reminds many of Eöl, the Dark Elf in *The Silmarillion*. Once again, it should be noted that Tolkien had a certain tendency to draw on ancient traditions preserved in fragmentary states. The coherent and complete aspect of a myth may have

5   Tolkien, 'Chaucer as a Philologist: The Reeve's Tale', in the journal *Transactions of the Philological Society,* 1934, pp. 1–70.

6   John Bowers, *Tolkien's Lost Chaucer,* Oxford University Press, 2019.

7   Trans. note: Edward R. Haymes, translator, *The Saga of Thidrek of Bern,* Garland, 1988.

interested him less given that it offered him fewer opportunities to construct his own sub-creation from old and traditional elements.

There are spectacles of nature that subdue us, that mark us. The laughter of Hephaestus, all-powerful, fascinates us, and reminds us of the power of the heavenly worlds. And Horace sings,

> Remiss and an infrequent worshiper of the gods, I strayed in pursuit of senseless wisdom; now I am forced to set sail back again and retrace my wandering steps. For Jupiter, often cleaving the clouds with flashes of lightning, has driven his thundering horses and swift chariot across a clear sky, until it had shaken the dull earth, the wandering rivers, the river Styx, the horrid seat of hateful Taenarus, and the heights of Atlas' mountain. A god is able to replace the lowest with the highest, to raise the humble and to humble the lofty. And greedy Fortune, with her clattering noise, delights in snatching a crown and replacing it elsewhere.[8]

This is the lesson that we must probably learn from the story of the sinking of the isle of Númenor in *The Silmarillion* at the end of the Second Age. This cataclysm is the consequence of the madness of its inhabitants and their quest for immortality, which reaches a climax when King Ar-Pharazôn, in an excess of hubris and under the yoke of Sauron, launches an armada against Valinor, the Undying Lands where the gods reside. Because of this final sacrilege, Manwë, the most powerful of the Valar, appeals to Eru, the supreme entity, who intervenes directly to make the isle of Númenor and its inhabitants disappear under the waves. This disaster, as Tolkien himself said, is 'a special variety of the Atlantis tradition. That seems to me so fundamental to "mythical history" ... that some version of it would have to come in.'[9] There is no need to reread Plato's *Timaeus* or *Critias* to see the parallels here. The *fall* of Númenor is at once an expression of a physical disaster — the world's shape is changed: formerly flat, it becomes round — and a metaphysical disaster, which recalls the

---

8   Horace, *Odes*, book I, ode 34. Trans. note: Translation of the Latin is my own.

9   Tolkien, *Letters*, no. 154.

destruction of Sodom and Gomorrah or the expulsion of the first parents from the Garden of Eden. It is an outrage caused in part by too great a material and military-technical nature, by a tireless urge to conquer. This downfall is again the result of hubris touching upon the sacred. Wanting to be equal to the gods is the ultimate sin. Also, Ilúvatar, the father of everything, intervenes as a demiurge, harnessing nature to punish Men. His act of superb power is due to divine ecology. To make the madness of the Númenóreans disappear under a gigantic wave and to give way to the calm movement of water is the aspiration.

The Technical Alienation of Isengard

The submersion of Númenor in some respects recalls the flood of Isengard during the War of the Ring.

While the armies of Saruman, a wizard seduced by Sauron, march into Rohan and fight at the Battle of Helm's Deep against the army of King Théoden, the Ents of Fangorn, who are spirits of the forest with the appearance of trees, at the same time assault the fortress of Isengard and flood it with the waters of the river Isen. The word *ent* means 'giant' in Old English, in the sense of an enigmatic race that is traditionally thought to be responsible for all sorts of massive ancient works in tradition (*enta geweorc*):

The precincts of the city have crumbled and the work of giants is rotting away. ('The Ruin', line 2)[10]
The old work of giants stood empty. ('The Wanderer', line 87)[11]

---

10 Trans. note: Bradley, 'The Ruin' in *Anglo-Saxon Poetry*, Everyman's Library, 1982, p. 402.

11 Trans. note: translation mine. The author is trying to highlight the Old English noun *ent* (plural genitive *enta*) and states that these structures were attributed to this race of giants. This line in Old English reads *eald enta geweorc idlu stodon*. Literally, 'old of giants work, empty [they] stood'. Bradley's translation, which is normally excellent, opts for 'the ancient gigantic structures stood desolate' (p. 324 in *Anglo-Saxon Poetry*, 1982), which somewhat disguises the

The first verses of 'Maxims II' — a gnomic poem — associate the word
ent with that of *orðanc* (Tolkien's name for the tower of Isengard):

> The king must rule over a realm. Cities are conspicuous from afar, those
> which there are on this earth, the ingenious constructions of giants [*orðanc
> enta geweorc*].[12]

Isengard means 'iron enclosure' in Old English and *Orðanc* means
'ingenious mind'. These names designate well the nature of the place
that evolves, during the War of the Ring, into a countryside destroyed
by human development.

> Once it had been green and filled with avenues, and groves of fruitful trees,
> watered by streams that flowed from the mountain to a lake. But no green
> thing grew there in the latter days of Saruman. The roads were paved with
> stone-flags, dark and hard; and beside their borders instead of trees there
> marched long lines of pillars, some of marble, some of copper and of iron,
> joined by heavy chains.[13]

The result is a terrifying description of a world oriented toward the
most sinister technology, driven by warlike ambitions and subjugation.

> [The shafts in the ground] were covered by low mounds and domes of
> stone, so that in the moonlight the Ring of Isengard looked like a graveyard
> of unquiet dead. For the ground trembled. The shafts ran down by many
> slopes and spiral stairs to caverns far under; there Saruman had treasuries,
> store-houses, armouries, smithies, and great furnaces. Iron wheels revolved
> there endlessly, and hammers thudded. At night plumes of vapour steamed
> from the vents, lit from beneath with red light, or blue, or venomous
> green.[14]

---

noun *enta* by making it an adjective. I have rendered a more literal translation
of this verse to highlight the noun.

12 Trans. note: Bradley, 'Maxims II' in *Anglo-Saxon Poetry*, Everyman's Library,
1982, p. 523.

13 Tolkien, *The Two Towers*, in the chapter 'The Road to Isengard', Houghton
Mifflin, 1965, p. 160.

14 Ibid.

In the face of this technological alienation, the Ents, the tree-herders, protect the great forest of Fangorn from any outside aggression which they might suffer from the enemy. As Walter Aubrig rightly points out, 'They can achieve this mission with considerable force and violence... Tolkien has inserted here a very large part of the affection that he himself had for trees, and of his disgust for businesses engaged in deforestation. As he confided in a letter from June 1972:[15] "In all my works I take the part of trees as against all their enemies." ... It is significant that, in the world of Arda, wild nature has a voice, an active incarnation, capable of defending itself, but even more, it is able to play a role in the narrative.'[16]

This effective way of working in the world of trees hearkens back to the purest Western tradition.[17] That of the forest as a special place for encounters with danger, whether with wrongdoers, with fabulous creatures, or with the vegetation itself. In mediaeval literature, it is accepted that the forest world is, if not neutral, somewhat hostile to man. It is in and against the forest that men are established. Robert Harrison argues that the West cleared its space in the heart of the forests.[18] So, with the capture of Isengard by the Ents, Tolkien revives here a motif that is found in many ancient texts. The author also brings in the Huorns — Ents that returned to a wild state, the state of trees. Fierce toward bipedal beings, they especially hate Orcs. On the last day of the Battle of Helm's Deep, the Huorns, who have moved, form a veritable forest in order to put the brood of evil to an end. No

---

15   Tolkien, *Letters*, no. 339.

16   Walter Aubrig, 'Tolkien et la question de la technique', in *J. R. R. Tolkien, Nouvelle École*, p. 66.

17   Robert Harrison, *Forests: The Shadow of Civilization*, University of Chicago Press, 1993. [Trans. note: Berger cites this author in its French translation, *Forêts: Essai sur l'imaginaire occidental*, translated by Florence Naugrette, Flammarion, 1992.]

18   Ibid.

one survives crossing that forest, made up of fighting trees, and here again is a motif well known in mythology.[19]

Tolkien's strong criticism of the modernisation, mechanisation, and industrialisation of the world, in his work decorated with traditional elements drawn from the riches of our civilisation, bears witness to an ecological way of thinking. In a letter dated 6 October 1944, Tolkien wrote to his son: 'If a ragnarök would burn all the slums and gas-works, and shabby garages, and long arc-lit suburbs, it could for me burn all the works of art — and I'd go back to trees.'[20] We are not far from Ernst Jünger's 'Recourse to the Forest'.[21]

The Happy Medium of the Hobbits

Between the madness of men dedicated to the cult of the machine and Nature — wild, autonomous, and conscious of its destiny —, Tolkien develops an ecology of imagination that is embodied by the people of the Hobbits. The material is of paramount importance. We must remember that *The Lord of the Rings* opens with a prologue that describes these strange creatures and their morals. In a few lines, Tolkien paints a portrait of their essential characteristics:

> Hobbits are an unobtrusive but very ancient people, more numerous formerly than they are today; for they love peace and quiet and good tilled earth: a well-ordered and well-farmed countryside was their favourite haunt. They do not and did not understand or like machines more complicated than a forge-bellows, a water-mill, or a hand-loom, though they were skilful with tools.[22]

---

19 Take, for example, the B version of the death of Cú Chulainn in the Irish tradition.

20 Trans. note: Tolkien, *Letters*, no. 83.

21 Trans. note: Ernst Jünger, *Der Waldgang*, 1951. The essay deals with the question of how people respond to catastrophe.

22 Trans. note: Tolkien, *The Fellowship of the Ring*, Houghton Mifflin, 1965, p. 10.

This people, in Middle-earth, cannot be defined as a civilisation of materialism. This contrast, in many ways, leaves this world of small people out of history. Events related to the Ring, however, show that they are endowed with the greatest courage. Hobbit culture, while not materialist, nevertheless possesses great refinement and considerable wealth. Hobbits have an attitude resolutely turned toward the exaltation of life in all its forms. Their lives are punctuated by festivities and the seasons. Among the Hobbit celebrations, the most emblematic is Yule, the winter solstice, which we first know by way of Germanic tradition. In many ways, the inhabitants of the Shire seem to hold the secret of serenity of which Martin Heidegger talked about. Their earthly way of life is fully ordered along the cosmos, based in nature, in accordance with the elements, again close to a Heideggerian conception of *habitat*, which is conceivable only if it is founded within the *quadripartite* that brings together the fundamental benchmarks of existence itself (earth and sky, mortals and divinities).[23] The Hobbits, in their simplicity, have an essential relationship to the world, which lies in the harmony between nature and culture. A happy medium portrayed with depth and sincerity by Tolkien, who displays here an ecological vision supported by imagination.

---

23 Martin Heidegger, 'Bauen Wohnen Denken', *Gesamtausgabe 7*, Vittorio Klostermann, 2000, pp. 145–165.

CHAPTER V

AS A DEFENCE OF
EUROPEAN CIVILISATION

HE MORE INSPIRATION ARISES, the more myth comes to life, and the more intense realism becomes.

Throughout his work, Tolkien implicitly develops a literary theory of the myth of creation, like a vast fresco unveiled to modern man, where intertwined motifs hearken back, through tradition, to the height of our ancient civilisation. The musicality of the author is endowed with a magical force inherent in ancient traditions: 'Let us think of these meaningless sayings and incantations which, of an undoubted curative virtue, have been preserved in the people and resonate like the calls of the spirits and the gods.'[1] These scores, which are difficult to decipher and scattered throughout the work, are nevertheless, against all expectations, familiar to us. In his own way, turned toward the imaginary, Tolkien is a custodian of a tradition that he passes down to us, for we must remember that the author portrays himself as a translator of tales and legends — those of *The Hobbit*, *The Lord of the Rings*, and *The Silmarillion*, compiled by Bilbo, Frodo, and Sam — that he discovered

---

1   Stefan George, *Feuilles pour l'art 1892–1919*, trans. L. Lehnen, Paris, Les Belles Lettres, 2012. Here the German poet speaks of the art of sound in the work of Stéphane Mallarmé.

in the *Red Book of Westmarch*, a set of manuscripts whose name is reminiscent of the *Red Book of Hergest*, a codex written in Welsh at the turn of the 14th century.

A word on the term *tradition*. Tradition is a matter of choice: either to pass it on, to ensure its succession, and to keep the heritage alive, or to let it disappear in the face of nihilism. If there is no longer any tradition, we renounce who we are and we leave the field free to all the excesses that the world generates on a daily basis. Such is the inevitable and necessary reaction of the Free Peoples of Middle-earth against Sauron and his minions. In the manner of Elves, Men, Dwarves, Hobbits, or Ents, it is up to us, individually or collectively, to defend our 'inner citadels', to use a phrase from Marc Aurèle, to hold firm the helm of the ship in the trough of the wave, to keep lit the last flicker of light in the darkness of the storm, to hope for a few rays of light in the dark fray. So, always, we will continue to exist as long as hope has not faded. The enemy will not triumph as long as tradition remains, as long as there are people in the world capable of holding up the full weight of a legacy. Renouncing one's land is an unthinkable idea, whether one is a Man of Gondor or a simple Hobbit. 'Where there is a will, there is a way', said William of Orange. Therefore, it is important not to 'burn our ships', as did the Elf Fëanor who, in *The Silmarillion*, wants to pursue Morgoth, the thief of the Silmarils — jewels that contain the reflection of the original light — as far as Middle-earth.

Crossing over from the Undying Lands requires ships and Fëanor seeks to convince the Teleri of the maritime city of Alqualondë to join him, or at least to give up their ships. The king of the city refuses and Fëanor gathers his army to take the vessels by force. In this way, the first fratricidal slaughter is committed in the world of Arda. After taking the ships and arriving in Middle-earth, Fëanor sets fire to the ships, making it impossible to return to their native shore. The link is broken and tradition is no longer. The gods turned away from the path of life. The outcome can only be tragic, and *The Silmarillion* depicts this decline with a strong seriousness. Should we, in the manner of Fëanor, renounce our origins in order to sink into a sad madness with a fatal end? Or should we, like the Hobbit in love with his land and the traditions that punctuate his daily life, undoubtedly frightened by the idea of seeing his dwelling fall prey to flame and fire, take control of our destiny, perhaps despite ourselves, for a higher cause? Such is the teaching of Tolkien which imposes on our consciences. What are we to do? To transmit or to disappear.

The Fall of the City

Tolkien had a solid Greco-Latin education[2] and a sure familiarity with the mythology and heroic poetry of that European tradition. It is therefore not surprising that important themes of his *Legendarium* originated in that tradition. Much like the Germanic or Celtic elements, the source is sometimes obvious: thus, the motif of Prometheus in chains when dealing with heroes who defied the power of Morgoth. This is taken up twice in *The Silmarillion*: the story of Maedhros, the son of Fëanor, and in the story of Húrin. But the major motifs concern the destruction of large cities. Isabelle Pantin writes, 'Indeed, the corpus of Tolkien's *Legendarium*, which spans three ages, is a vision of the development and the decline of civilisations, grasped at the encounter between myth and history. Although this represents a world that is inhabited only sparsely, cities are key elements. And in order to find myths for these cities, Tolkien had to turn more toward the Mediterranean and not the North.'[3] It is necessary to mention this line

---

2   Trans. note: Berger uses *culture* here — 'une solide culture gréco-latine' — but this can only be true in an academic sense, not in terms of Tolkien's ancestry or place of residence. I have used *education* to reflect that distinction.

3   Isabelle Pantin, 'L'ombre de Troie dans l'œuvre de Tolkien',' *L'Antiquité dans l'imaginaire contemporain*, Paris, Classiques Garnier, 2014, p. 156.

taken from Tolkien's correspondence: 'There cannot be any "story" without a fall — all stories are ultimately about the fall …'[4]

This theme is salient throughout the history of Arda. In this way Númenor is swallowed up, Gondolin fallen — this story owes much to the influence of William Morris — and Minas Tirith almost taken. The theme of the fall of a city naturally is inspired by the Greco-Latin world. The sacking of Troy, especially. Recall that, according to Apollodorus, the major challenge during the siege of the city is, for the Achaeans, in stealing the Palladium. This artifact, shaped by Athena, which represents her with the aegis and javelin, confers impregnability to the Trojan city. The Greeks must therefore seize the sacred statue to bring down Troy. According to Greek tradition, it is stolen by Odysseus and Diomedes, who bring it back to their ship. This legendary episode calls to mind the heroic pair Frodo and Sam, who must go to the enemy, in Mordor, to throw the One Ring into the volcano in order to defeat Sauron. Asymmetric warfare, led by trickery, allows victory.

Among the many battles related in *The Lord of the Rings*, that of the Pelennor Fields, in front of the walls of the white city of Minas Tirith, deserves special attention. The men of Gondor bravely defend the city, but are soon unable to prevent Mordor's troops from setting up a siege. Very quickly, the walls that surround Minas Tirith fall one by one under the fire of catapults and incendiaries. The gate of the city is soon smashed by a mighty battering ram. The armies enter the city, led by the Witch-king of Angmar, Sauron's second-in-command, Lord of the Nazgûl. The wizard Gandalf stands up to him; every moment of resistance counts. At the same time, as a *eucatastrophe*, to use the term conceptualised by Tolkien, the reinforcements of Rohan arrive with King Théoden at their head. At the cost of many lives, the battle ends in a defeat for the forces of Mordor. The debacle prevents the fall of the city *in extremis*. The scale and importance of this war story have prompted comparisons with real historical events. In an earlier footnote, we mentioned the parallel with the Battle of the Catalaunian

---

4   Tolkien, *Letters*, no. 131.

Plains by following the opinion — with Franz Liszt's *Hunnenschlacht* in mind — of Tom Shippey, one of the greatest Tolkien scholars. Wayne G. Hammond and Christina Scull, two other scholarly commentators on the work of the Oxford professor, propose an alternative. They see in this episode an inspiration from the siege of Constantinople in 1453 and that of Vienna in 1683, recalling Tolkien's own comparison between Minas Tirith and the Great City: 'In the south Gondor rises to a peak of power, almost reflecting Númenor, and then fades slowly to decayed Middle Age, a kind of proud, venerable, but increasingly impotent Byzantium. The watch on Mordor is relaxed. The pressure of the Easterlings and Southrons increases.'[5] The city never falls into the hands of the enemy as long as hope remains, like an unwavering feeling:

> "That is one thing that Men call 'hope'", said Finrod. "*Amdir* we call it, 'looking up'. But there is another which is founded deeper. *Estel* we call it, that is 'trust'".[6]

For an Ultimate Rebirth

Tolkien confers on his *Legendarium* a singular musicality, punctuated by traditional leitmotifs that reveal themselves to us, like reminiscences, in the manner of mnemonic formulas. Such inspiration, translated through Tolkien, is thus more firmly anchored in us. We remember that Númenor recalls Atlantis, and vice versa. There is an interdependence between the rhythm of life and culture. The author delves into the sources of life and human existence. Tolkien anchors the poetic word in an archetypal and mythical understanding, blending speech, image, and rhythm — a finely crafted mosaic that acts upon us at the time of the unveiling of a strangely new yet familiar civilisation: 'A new degree of culture occurs when one or more original minds reveal

---

5   Wayne Hammond and Christina Scull, *The Lord of the Rings: A Reader's Companion*, Houghton Mifflin Company, 2005, pp. 569–571. See also Tolkien, *Letters*, no. 131.

6   Tolkien, *Morgoth's Ring*, Houghton Mifflin Company, 1993, p. 320.

their life-rhythm, which is taken on first by a community and then by a larger section of the population. The original spirit does not act by its doctrine, but by its rhythm: doctrine is later made by the disciples.[7]

Little by little, as the work of the weavers takes shape, a monumental tapestry rises before us. What is blurry now becomes clearer. The contours and shapes become more precise. We finally take a step back, after being thrown into it, to contemplate with new eyes the whole piece that comes to life before our fixed gaze. We can hardly believe it. Middle-earth, this enclosure of men dear to the Germanic imagination, is in reality a projection of our world, that of our Europe, into more remote times. In the margins of a 1958 letter, Tolkien wrote, 'I imagine the gap [between the end of the Third Age and today] to be about 6000 years: that is we are now at the end of the Fifth Age, if the Ages were of about the same length as S.A.[8] and T.A. But they have, I think, quickened; and I imagine we are actually at the end of the Sixth Age, or in the Seventh.'[9] The author, as he further explains, built an 'imaginary *time*, but kept my feet on my own mother-earth for *place*.'[10] The link between Middle-earth and our world remains, and is reborn every moment for the enthusiastic reader.

It is up to European man to know his modern mythology and the heroes related to it. Tolkien, like an 'Anglo-Saxon bard', as Wystan Hugh Auden called him,[11] is one of those noble heralds who have brought our civilisational wealth to its pinnacle. May his work, as a new founding text for our identity, allow us to maintain the sacred fire.

---

7   Stefan George, cited above, p. 94.

8   Trans. note: S.A. and T.A. stand for the *Second Age* and *Third Age*, respectively.

9   Tolkien, *Letters*, no. 211.

10 Ibid.

11 'For those who have learned to hope: a lot of us are grateful for / What J. R. R. Tolkien has done / As bard to Anglo-Saxon.' Wystan Hugh Auden, 'A Short Ode to a Philologist', *English and Medieval Studies. Presented to J. R. R. Tolkien on the Occasion of his Seventieth Birthday*, George Allen & Unwin, 1962, pp. 11–12.

BIBLIOGRAPHY FOR
FURTHER READING

Charles Delattre, *Le cycle de l'anneau: De Minos à Tolkien*, Belin, 2009.

Michaël Devaux (dir.), *Tolkien, les racines du légendaire, cahier d'études tolkieniennes* no. 2, Ad Solem, 2003.

François-Marin Fleutot, *Les Mythes du Seigneur des Anneaux*, Le Rocher, 2003.

J. R. R. Tolkien, Nouvelle École, no. 70, 2021.

Isabelle Pantin, *Tolkien et ses légendes: Une expérience en fiction*, C.N.R.S. Éditions, 2009.

Charles Ridoux, *Tolkien: Le Chant du Monde*, Encrage, 2004.

Tom Shippey, *The Road to Middle-Earth: How J. R. R. Tolkien Created a New Mythology*, HarperCollins, 1992.

Tom Shippey, *Roots and Branches: Selected Papers on Tolkien*, Walking Tree Publishers, 2007.

Rudolf Simek, *La Terre du Milieu: Tolkien et la mythologie germano-scandinave*, trans. by M. Brecq and E. Ebnöther, foreword by L. Carruthers, Passés composés, 2019.

L'INSTITUT ILIADE FOR LONG EUROPEAN MEMORY

L'Institut Iliade for Long European Memory, based in France, was born from an observation. Europe is but a shadow of her former self. Replaced by outsiders, confused by having lost their bearing and their pride, Europeans have abandoned the reins of their common destiny to people other than themselves. Europeans no longer remember. Why? Because amongst the current elite — whether at school, university, or in the media — no one passes down to them the cultural wealth of which they are the inheritors.

Contrary to this moribund current, L'Institut Iliade has given itself the task of participating in the renewal of the cultural grandeur of Europe and in aiding Europeans' reappropriation of their own identity. Facing the Great Erasure of culture, we intend to work for the Great Awakening of European consciousness and to help prepare Europe for a new renaissance — one of identity, freedom, and power.

L'Institut Iliade's calling is threefold:

- To train young men and young women concerned about their history to always build. To make them the avantgarde of the renaissance for which the Institut calls: men and women capable of giving to civic and political action that cultural and metapolitical dimension which is indispensable. Their motto: to put themselves at the service of a community of destiny, which risks disappearing if it is not taken in hand. Armed with a strong culture relating to European traditions and values, they learn to discern that the adventure that awaits them entails risks and self-sacrifice, but also enthusiasm and joy.

- To promote a radical and alternative vision of the world contrary to the dogmas of universalism, egalitarianism, and 'diversity'. Using all available means, the Institut develops concepts and ammunition to understand and fight the modern world.

- To gather together, especially — but not only — in France, those who refuse to submit and who are inspired daily by the Homeric triad as described by Dominique Venner: nature as the base, excellence as the goal, beauty as the horizon.

L'Institut Iliade's originality, especially with the aim of reformulating and updating knowledge, lies in tying together the seriousness of its content with ease of learning for the greater public, the objective being to demonstrate an authentic pedagogy, and to act in complementary or supportive ways with other initiatives having the same goal.

L'Institut Iliade's action takes place across various channels:

- A cadre school of the European Rebirth, which every year brings together trainees from a wide variety of backgrounds and is already seeing citizens from other European countries participate;

- an annual colloquium — made up of academics, politicians, writers, journalists, and association officials from all over Europe — that meets in Paris to discuss strong and challenging themes, such as 'The Aesthetic Universe of Europeans', 'Facing the Migratory Assault', 'Transmit or Disappear', 'Nature as Base — for an Ecology of Place', 'Beyond the Market — Economy at the Service of Peoples';

- the publication of works — designed as beacons to enlighten readers' thoughts and guide them toward the reconquest of their identity — within several collections, made available in the widest array of languages and European countries;

- artistic exhibitions on the fringes of contemporary artistic trends, allowing the public to take a fresh look at art and rooted creation;

- an incubator for ideas, businesses, and associations to support and help the greatest number of projects — with quality and sustainability criteria — across all fields of civil society (culture, commerce, etc.) that seek to impose a rooted vision of the world and an alternative to the current system, while prioritising structures and projects making an impact in real life;

- an active presence on social media, allowing us to reach new audiences (through videos, publications, annual events, and news presentations), centred around a website that functions as much as a resource hub as it does as a platform for exchanges and debate, notably offering an ideal library of more than five hundred works, a European primer, a dictionary of quotations, and turnkey itineraries for visiting and hiking the prominent places of European memory.

Education through history:
L'Institut Iliade endeavours to uphold in every circumstance the richness and singularity of our heritage in order to draw forth the source and the resources of a serene, but determined, affirmation of our identity, both national and European. In line with the thought and deeds of Dominique Venner, the Institut accords in all its activities an essential place to history, both as a matrix of deep meditation on the future as well as a place of the unexpected, where anything is possible.

Concerning Europe, it seems as though we will be forced to rise up and face immense challenges and fearsome catastrophes even beyond those posed by immigration. These hardships will present the opportunity for both a rebirth and a rediscovery of ourselves. I believe in those qualities that are specific to the European people, qualities currently in a state of dormancy. I believe in our active individuality, our inventiveness, and in the awakening of our energy. This awakening will undoubtedly come. When? I do not know, but I am positive that it will take place.

— Dominique Venner, *The Shock of History*
Arktos Media, London, 2015

Follow L'Institut Iliade at
www.institut-iliade.com
linktr.ee/InstitutILIADE

OTHER BOOKS PUBLISHED BY ARKTOS

SRI DHARMA PRAVARTAKA ACHARYA — *The Dharma Manifesto*

JOAKIM ANDERSEN — *Rising from the Ruins*

WINSTON C. BANKS — *Excessive Immigration*

ALAIN DE BENOIST — *Beyond Human Rights*
Carl Schmitt Today
The Indo-Europeans
Manifesto for a European Renaissance
On the Brink of the Abyss
The Problem of Democracy
Runes and the Origins of Writing
View from the Right (vol. 1–3)

ARTHUR MOELLER VAN DEN BRUCK — *Germany's Third Empire*

MATT BATTAGLIOLI — *The Consequences of Equality*

KERRY BOLTON — *The Perversion of Normality*
Revolution from Above
Yockey: A Fascist Odyssey

ISAC BOMAN — *Money Power*

CHARLES WILLIAM DAILEY — *The Serpent Symbol in Tradition*

RICARDO DUCHESNE — *Faustian Man in a Multicultural Age*

ALEXANDER DUGIN — *Ethnos and Society*
Ethnosociology
Eurasian Mission
The Fourth Political Theory
The Great Awakening vs the Great Reset
Last War of the World-Island
Political Platonism
Putin vs Putin
The Rise of the Fourth Political Theory
The Theory of a Multipolar World

EDWARD DUTTON — *Race Differences in Ethnocentrism*

MARK DYAL — *Hated and Proud*

CLARE ELLIS — *The Blackening of Europe*

KOENRAAD ELST — *Return of the Swastika*

JULIUS EVOLA — *The Bow and the Club*
Fascism Viewed from the Right
A Handbook for Right-Wing Youth
Metaphysics of Power
Metaphysics of War
The Myth of the Blood
Notes on the Third Reich
The Path of Cinnabar
Recognitions
A Traditionalist Confronts Fascism

OTHER BOOKS PUBLISHED BY ARKTOS

GUILLAUME FAYE	*Archeofuturism*
	Archeofuturism 2.0
	The Colonisation of Europe
	Convergence of Catastrophes
	Ethnic Apocalypse
	A Global Coup
	Prelude to War
	Sex and Deviance
	Understanding Islam
	Why We Fight
DANIEL S. FORREST	*Suprahumanism*
ANDREW FRASER	*Dissident Dispatches*
	The WASP Question
GÉNÉRATION IDENTITAIRE	*We are Generation Identity*
PETER GOODCHILD	*The Taxi Driver from Baghdad*
	The Western Path
PAUL GOTTFRIED	*War and Democracy*
PETR HAMPL	*Breached Enclosure*
PORUS HOMI HAVEWALA	*The Saga of the Aryan Race*
LARS HOLGER HOLM	*Hiding in Broad Daylight*
	Homo Maximus
	Incidents of Travel in Latin America
	The Owls of Afrasiab
RICHARD HOUCK	*Liberalism Unmasked*
A. J. ILLINGWORTH	*Political Justice*
ALEXANDER JACOB	*De Naturae Natura*
JASON REZA JORJANI	*Closer Encounters*
	Faustian Futurist
	Iranian Leviathan
	Lovers of Sophia
	Novel Folklore
	Prometheism
	Prometheus and Atlas
	Uber Man
	World State of Emergency
HENRIK JONASSON	*Sigmund*
VINCENT JOYCE	*The Long Goodbye*
RUUBEN KAALEP & AUGUST MEISTER	*Rebirth of Europe*
RODERICK KAINE	*Smart and SeXy*
PETER KING	*Here and Now*
	Keeping Things Close
	On Modern Manners

OTHER BOOKS PUBLISHED BY ARKTOS

JAMES KIRKPATRICK	*Conservatism Inc.*
LUDWIG KLAGES	*The Biocentric Worldview*
	Cosmogonic Reflections
	The Science of Character
ANDREW KORYBKO	*Hybrid Wars*
PIERRE KREBS	*Guillaume Faye: Truths & Tributes*
	Fighting for the Essence
JULIEN LANGELLA	*Catholic and Identitarian*
JOHN BRUCE LEONARD	*The New Prometheans*
STEPHEN PAX LEONARD	*The Ideology of Failure*
	Travels in Cultural Nihilism
WILLIAM S. LIND	*Reforging Excalibur*
	Retroculture
PENTTI LINKOLA	*Can Life Prevail?*
H. P. LOVECRAFT	*The Conservative*
NORMAN LOWELL	*Imperium Europa*
RICHARD LYNN	*Sex Differences in Intelligence*
JOHN MACLUGASH	*The Return of the Solar King*
CHARLES MAURRAS	*The Future of the Intelligentsia*
	& For a French Awakening
JOHN HARMON MCELROY	*Agitprop in America*
MICHAEL O'MEARA	*Guillaume Faye and the Battle of Europe*
	New Culture, New Right
MICHAEL MILLERMAN	*Beginning with Heidegger*
BRIAN ANSE PATRICK	*The NRA and the Media*
	Rise of the Anti-Media
	The Ten Commandments of Propaganda
	Zombology
TITO PERDUE	*The Bent Pyramid*
	Journey to a Location
	Lee
	Morning Crafts
	Philip
	The Sweet-Scented Manuscript
	William's House (vol. 1–4)
JOHN K. PRESS	*The True West vs the Zombie Apocalypse*
RAIDO	*A Handbook of Traditional*
	Living (vol. 1–2)
CLAIRE RAE RANDALL	*The War on Gender*
STEVEN J. ROSEN	*The Agni and the Ecstasy*

OTHER BOOKS PUBLISHED BY ARKTOS

	The Jedi in the Lotus
RICHARD RUDGLEY	*Barbarians*
	Essential Substances
	Wildest Dreams
ERNST VON SALOMON	*It Cannot Be Stormed*
	The Outlaws
WERNER SOMBART	*Traders and Heroes*
PIERO SAN GIORGIO	*CBRN*
	Giuseppe
	Survive the Economic Collapse
SRI SRI RAVI SHANKAR	*Celebrating Silence*
	Know Your Child
	Management Mantras
	Patanjali Yoga Sutras
	Secrets of Relationships
GEORGE T. SHAW (ED.)	*A Fair Hearing*
FENEK SOLÈRE	*Kraal*
OSWALD SPENGLER	*The Decline of the West*
	Man and Technics
RICHARD STOREY	*The Uniqueness of Western Law*
TOMISLAV SUNIC	*Against Democracy and Equality*
	Homo Americanus
	Postmortem Report
	Titans are in Town
ASKR SVARTE	*Gods in the Abyss*
HANS-JÜRGEN SYBERBERG	*On the Fortunes and Misfortunes of Art in Post-War Germany*
ABIR TAHA	*Defining Terrorism*
	The Epic of Arya (2nd ed.)
	Nietzsche's Coming God, or the Redemption of the Divine
	Verses of Light
JEAN THIRIART	*Europe: An Empire of 400 Million*
BAL GANGADHAR TILAK	*The Arctic Home in the Vedas*
DOMINIQUE VENNER	*For a Positive Critique*
	The Shock of History
HANS VOGEL	*How Europe Became American*
MARKUS WILLINGER	*A Europe of Nations*
	Generation Identity
ALEXANDER WOLFHEZE	*Alba Rosa*
	Rupes Nigra